DANIEL AND THE LIONS

Daniel 6 for Children

Written by Larry Burgdorf
Illustrated by Natalia Vasquez

CONCORDIA PUBLISHING HOUSE · SAINT LOUIS

If lions had the gift of speech
There are some things that they could teach.
There is one cat especially
Who could tell much to you and me.

If he could talk, what would he say?
His story could be told this way:
"Long, long ago in Babylon
A lot of things were going on.

"I'd lived each day with my small crew
And did just what most lions do.
(You may well know, as an aside—
A crew of us is called a 'pride.')

"Then trappers came for us one day.
They caught us and took us away.
They showed us to the king and then
They put us in his lions' den.

"We all were very hungry when
They threw a man into our den.
Aha! I thought. *It's time to eat!*
My pride rushed forward for this treat.

"I later learned why he was here
Inside this place of raging fear.
His name was Daniel and he had
Some enemies who were quite mad.

"Daniel was honored by the king
Who gave him charge of everything.
Those men with jealousy and hate
Had tried to seal poor Daniel's fate.

"They hatched a plan and tricked the king,
Who signed a really rotten thing.
That awful law would not permit
A prayer to God one little bit.

"Now, anyone who disobeyed,
No matter to which god he prayed,
Would be arrested there and then
And thrown into our fearsome den.

"Well, Daniel knew it wasn't right.
He knew this law was done from spite.
He kept on praying anyway
To the true God, three times a day.

"His enemies were watching then.
They looked into his window when
They saw, to their malicious glee:
Someone was praying! It was he!

"They took him to the king who said,
'I surely don't want Daniel dead.'
"Those evil men then pointed out:
'He has to die without a doubt.'

"The king agreed that this was true
So there was nothing he could do.
He handed Daniel over then—
That's how he got into our den.

"As we were rushing for the feast
We couldn't touch him in the least.
God sent His angel here, and he
Was far more powerful than we.

"We couldn't hurt Daniel because
God closed our mouths and sheathed our claws.
So when the king came here to see,
Daniel was healthy as could be.

"I'm sure you're glad Daniel got free,
And you should be, but think of me!
You can imagine how I feel—
That day I missed a tasty meal!

"But it was all right, if you please—
Remember Daniel's enemies?
The king threw in those evil men,
So there was feasting in our den."

Dear Parents,

We are taught to obey the law. In fact, God demands it when He says to honor your father and your mother. Even kings must obey the law. (See Romans 13:1–2.)

Daniel had so impressed King Darius that he was appointed to one of the highest positions of power and authority in the kingdom. But he clearly broke the law when he prayed to God, and this infraction was punishable by death. Daniel's enemies had finally succeeded in defeating him, stripping him of his position and security.

In this story we learn that sometimes bad things do happen to good people. Sometimes even the most faithful Christians we know find themselves in a cold dark pit surrounded by hungry lions and with no hope of escape. But even then, God tells us, "Be watchful. Your adversary the devil prowls around like a roaring lion, seeking someone to devour. Resist him, firm in your faith" (1 Peter 5:8–9).

Even if this story had ended differently, Daniel would still be a model for us because his faith in the one true God never wavered. If you feel it is appropriate, talk with your child about Bible stories in which God's faithful didn't come out alive (John the Baptist, Stephen). The lesson that Daniel and these other people teach is that God sent Someone—our Savior, Jesus—to pull us out of the pit and into the light of eternal day.

To Him be the glory!

The Editor